Captain Cook

Alan Blackwood

Illustrated by Richard Hook

The Bookwright Press
New York · 1987

Great Lives

William Shakespeare
Queen Elizabeth II
Anne Frank
Martin Luther King, Jr.
Helen Keller
Ferdinand Magellan
Mother Teresa
Louis Braille
John Lennon
John F. Kennedy
Florence Nightingale
Elvis Presley
Captain Cook
Gandhi

First published in the
United States in 1987 by
The Bookwright Press
387 Park Avenue South
New York, NY 10016

First published in 1986 by
Wayland (Publishers) Ltd
61 Western Road, Hove
East Sussex, BN3 1JD, England

ISBN 0–531–18091–3
Library of Congress Catalog Card Number: 86 70989

Phototypeset by Kalligraphics Ltd, Redhill, Surrey
Printed in Italy by G. Canale & C.S.p.A., Turin

Contents

A farmhand's son

James Cook was born in a village in Yorkshire, England on October 27, 1728. His father worked on a farm, and the family lived in a small, earthen-walled cottage on the edge of the moors. Young Cook was lucky, because the local landowner took an interest in him and paid for his schooling. He learned to read and write, and showed a flair for arithmetic. At the age of 17, he became an assistant in a local grocery store – a big step up the ladder of success for a farm laborer's son. But not far away was the port of Whitby on the Yorkshire coast, and young Cook longed to go to sea.

At the age of 18, Cook was a big, strong young man, and nearly 2 meters (over 6 feet) tall, which was very large for those days. He joined a local coal ship, or collier, which sailed along the east coast of England, calling at ports and harbors. Cook was eager and quick to learn, and was soon promoted to mate, or second in command, of the ship. The North Sea, with its strong tides, dense fogs and high winds, was a difficult and dangerous place in which to sail. But young Cook had become a very skilled

The two-room cottage in Marton-in-Cleveland where James Cook was born in 1728.

seaman. While other ships sank or ran aground on rocks and sandbanks, his sturdy collier always came safely back to Whitby. He was promised command of a new ship, and his prospects looked excellent. Then, suddenly, Britain was at war with France, and Cook went off to fight for his country.

As a boy, Cook used to visit the port of Whitby, and dreamed of going to sea.

The Navy

The Seven Years War (1756–63) was fought, in part, between Britain and France over possession of Canada. Cook joined the Royal Navy. Conditions aboard ship for ordinary sailors were terrible – bad food, wretched quarters and brutal discipline. Thanks to his skills and his will to succeed, Cook did not have to endure these conditions for long. He was made boatswain, or bo'sun, in charge of sails and rigging, on the 60-gun HMS *Eagle*, and got his first taste of action in the Bay of Biscay. He was soon promoted again, to ship's master in charge of navigation on HMS *Pembroke*, and sailed with the British fleet for Canada.

The French had a strong military garrison in Quebec, which stood on the Heights of Abraham, high above the St. Lawrence River. The wide, fast-flowing river was a navigator's nightmare of rocks and cross-

Cook led many patrols up the St. Lawrence River, charting a safe channel for the British warships.

currents. Several times before, a British squadron had tried to sail up the St. Lawrence to attack Quebec, and had come to grief. The French were sure they could hold the town, and Canada, against any new British attack.

But they had reckoned without Cook. He led patrols up and down the river, charting every hazard, and marking a channel for the warships to follow. Then one dark night in 1759, he guided the fleet safely to a point where British troops could land and take the enemy by surprise. Under General Wolfe, they captured Quebec, and won Canada for Britain. They could not have done this without the Royal Navy, and especially the help of ship's master James Cook.

These instruments were used by Cook to carry out his surveys of the St. Lawrence River in Canada.

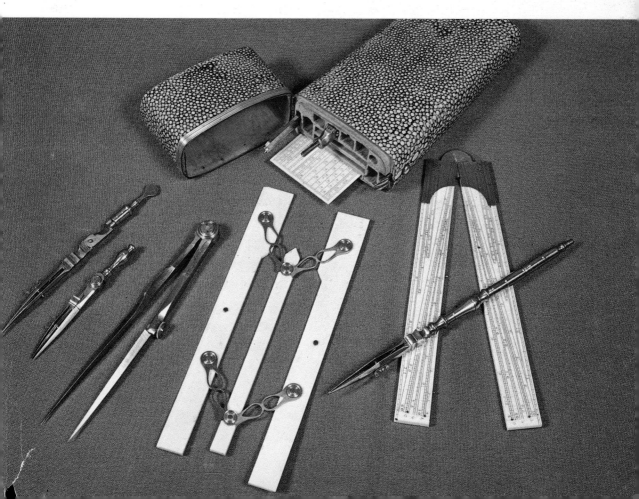

Taking command

After the war, Cook married a shopkeeper's daughter, Elizabeth Batts, and set up housekeeping in London. But at 34 years of age, he could not think of settling down. For several years he sailed to and from Newfoundland, charting its rocky coasts. Then in 1768 his big chance came.

The Navy was planning an expedition to the South Pacific Ocean. Its main objective was to find *Terra Australis* ("The Southern Land"), which scientists and geographers believed must exist to counter-balance the great land mass of Asia and Europe in the Northern Hemisphere. Explorers had been searching for this land ever since Ferdinand Magellan first sailed into the Pacific Ocean in 1520.

The expedition would also try to observe the transit, or movement, of the planet Venus across the sun; a rare event which the English astronomer Charles Halley (who gave his name to the famous comet) predicted would occur in 1769. It was thought that somewhere in the South Pacific would be a good place to make the observation.

Who would lead such an important voyage of discovery? Cook's outstanding seamanship was already well known, and his report on an eclipse of the sun, observed off the Newfoundland coast, had impressed the Royal Society, Britain's leading scientific institution. He was summoned to the Admiralty, handed his officer's commission, and as Lieutenant James Cook took command of the expedition's ship, HMS *Endeavour*.

Ferdinand Magellan (1480–1521) sailed into the Pacific in 1520 and set off the search for Terra Australis.

Outward bound

The *Endeavour* was not a warship, but a converted collier, very like the ship on which Cook had served his apprenticeship. Just over 32 meters (104 feet) in length, she was not designed for speed, but was strongly built, with plenty of storage space – ideal for a long voyage.

In preparing for the expedition, Cook gave much thought to the health and well-being of his crew. He knew that damp and dirt bred disease, and so he took on board

Above *The* Endeavour *was a small ship, measuring only 32 meters (105 feet).*

barrels of vinegar, for regular scrubbing and cleaning of the ship's deck and cabins.

A balanced diet, in Cook's opinion, was just as important to health. Scurvy was a terrible sickness that afflicted thousands of sailors who lived on the traditional ship's fare of salted meat, cheese, biscuits, rum and beer. Cook believed that fresh food could prevent scurvy. So he took on board coops of hens, to provide fresh eggs and meat, and also onions and sauerkraut (pickled cabbage) as the most convenient forms of vegetables. The crew might not like sauerkraut, but Cook would make sure that they ate it.

In July 1768 the *Endeavour* set sail. Among her passengers were distinguished scientists, and astronomers, as well as zoologists and botanists anxious to study animal and plant life on the other side of the world. For much of the time, Cook followed the route taken by Magellan over two hundred years before – westward across the Atlantic, down the coast of South America, around Cape Horn and into the Pacific. Their first destination was the island of Tahiti.

From Tahiti to New Zealand

Maori war canoes were very swift, powered by up to a hundred oars.

In April 1769 the expedition arrived at the lovely tropical island of Tahiti, in the middle of the Pacific Ocean. There the astronomers set up their instruments, and under cloudless skies they made their observations of the transit of Venus across the sun. The crew of the *Endeavour* received a warm welcome from the native people, and spent a happy three months on the island.

In July the expedition set sail again, to begin the search for *Terra Australis*. For three months they sailed on, west and south, across the empty, gray-green ocean, until at last they sighted more land. They had reached New Zealand. Over a century before, in 1642, the Dutch explorer Abel Tasman had first charted a small stretch of the coast. Cook now began a thorough exploration, and in six months he had charted the coasts of two large islands, separated by the strait that now bears his name – Cook Strait.

The explorers also encountered the local inhabitants, the Maoris, who were quite different from the charming, easy going Tahitians. They were tough, brave warriors and they attacked Cook and his men with spears even though the seamen used firearms against them. Several were killed, much to Cook's regret, for he admired them. "The natives of this country," he wrote in his log book, "are a strong, well-made, active people, rather above the common size. Many of them live to a good old age." He also described their magnificent ocean-going canoes, which could carry up to a hundred people, and the remarkable body tattoos that some of the Maoris displayed.

Cook had the *Endeavour* careened – hauled partly ashore – so that her wooden hull could be scrubbed and repaired before leaving New Zealand. By this time the expedition had been in the Pacific for over a year.

Botany Bay

Cook planned to sail westward across the Indian Ocean and around the Cape of Good Hope, thus making a circumnavigation of the world. But his first priority was Australia (or New Holland as it was then called). Other explorers had charted stretches of the west and north coasts, and Tasman had sighted the island named after him – Tasmania.

Many species of plants found in Botany Bay were previously unknown in Europe. Above The newly-found Sopha Tetraptera. Left The beautiful red honeysuckle.

Cook was the first to map the east coast. From the deck of the *Endeavour*, the land looked flat, dry and empty – a great contrast to the mountains, forests and rivers of New Zealand. The local inhabitants – the Aborigines – were physically smaller than the Maoris and did not welcome Cook and his crew to their land.

But the expedition eventually landed, and the botanists were delighted with the number of different species of plants they found. Cook named the place Botany Bay, and it became the site of the first white settlements in years to come.

Proceeding northward up the coast, between the mainland and the Great Barrier Reef, the *Endeavour* was nearly shipwrecked. She struck a bank of coral, which ripped a large hole in her hull below the water line. The crew threw overboard guns and cannon balls, iron pots and pans, and even spare timbers and precious stores, in an effort to raise the ship in the water and set her free of the deadly coral. They then towed her through dangerous reefs and currents to the shore, where the damage was repaired. Only Cook's great experience, his calm nerve, and the discipline of his crew saved them from disaster.

Home – but not for long

The crew of the *Endeavour* sighted Land's End, Cornwall, in July 1771, and Cook was given a hero's welcome home. He had sailed around New Zealand (thus proving that it was not a part of *Terra Australis*), then up the east coast of Australia, charting over 8,000 km (5,000 miles) of previously unknown coastline. The expedition had also brought back much new information about the plant and animal life of the lands that had been visited.

Cook discusses the advantages of the chronometer as a navigational aid.

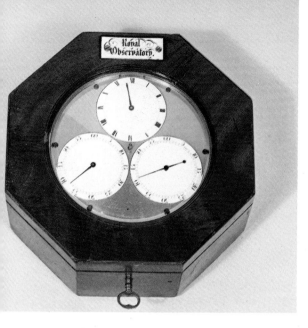

This chronometer, invented in 1774, was based on the one used by Cook, and proved to be a useful navigational instrument.

And although 38 of the 94 members of the voyage had died of tropical diseases, there had been hardly any sign of scurvy, thanks to Cook's ideas on diet and hygiene.

However, Cook was given little time to rest and relax at home. Plans were soon afoot for him to lead another search for *Terra Australis*, which was still thought to be somewhere quite apart from the newly-charted coasts of Australia.

As with the first expedition, there was a second objective. Every year, hundreds of ships lost their way through faulty navigation. A common cause of such failure was not knowing the time of day. Ordinary clocks of the period were operated by weights or a pendulum, and these did not work properly on board because of the ship's own motion. Recently, however, a new kind of timepiece called a chronometer had been invented which, it was hoped, would keep accurate time at sea. The Admiralty wanted Cook to test it out.

Cook was raised to the rank of commander, and given two new ships, the *Resolution* and the *Adventure*, both of which were larger than the *Endeavour*.

The Resolution *had a crew of about a hundred men, under Cook's command, as well as a number of scientists on board.*

The Antarctic

With Cook aboard the *Resolution* and Lieutenant Tobias Furneaux in charge of the *Adventure*, the expedition set sail in July 1772. This time they headed due south across the equator, past the Cape of Good Hope, and on into the uncharted waters of the Antarctic Ocean.

By this time it was December, and coming up to midsummer in the Southern Hemisphere. But the weather was still bad. "All the rigging covered with ice and the air excessive cold," Cook reported in his log. Blizzards lashed the two ships and icebergs threatened to strike and sink them. It was a hard time for the crews. They wore "fearnoughts" (jackets made of wool and thick canvas), and fur or woolen caps. But when they handled the rigging they had to keep their hands free, and frost bite, which could cause the loss of fingers, was a constant danger.

Undaunted, Cook and his companions became the first people to cross the Antarctic Circle. From that point they steered eastward, sailing south of Australia – with no sign of *Terra Australis* – to the southern tip of New Zealand.

Cook spent the next seven months in the calmer waters of the South Pacific, calling in at Tahiti, and charting the scattered islands of Polynesia.

Sad to say he found many of the islanders suffering from European diseases, which had been brought to Tahiti by the crew of the *Endeavour* when they first visited the island in 1769. Cook then headed south again. The *Resolution* and the *Adventure* lost contact in a storm, so Cook and his valiant crew went on alone, holding a south-easterly course that took them back over the Antarctic Circle. They pressed on until a solid barrier of ice blocked their way.

They had not found *Terra Australis*. Instead they had ventured farther south than any men before them, and had come very close to Antarctica, the coldest land on earth.

Lieutenant Tobias Furneaux (1735–81), a skilled sailor, took command of the Adventure *on Cook's second voyage.*

Pacific exploration

From the frozen wastes of the Antarctic Ocean, Cook sailed the *Resolution* north for several weeks. He wanted to take a sighting of Easter Island. This small Pacific island, in the midst of a vast expanse of empty sea, is one of the loneliest spots on earth. Cook wrote, "There is hardly an island in this sea which affords less refreshments and convenience for shipping than this does. Nature has hardly provided it with anything fit for man to eat or drink."

Cook and his crew saw the massive stone statues for which the island is famous. They stand on the grassy slopes of the island, and some of them are over 9 meters (30 feet) tall. It is thought that the statues are ancient burial stones of the Polynesian people who colonized most of the Pacific.

Between March and November 1774, Cook carried out further exploration of the Pacific. Briefly

The enormous statues on Easter Island are thought to be ancient burial stones.

Cook and his crews saw Tahitian warriors putting to sea in a formidable display.

visiting Tahiti, he witnessed the local war fleet putting to sea. The warriors, Cook recorded, "were dressed in a vast quantity of cloth, turbans, breastplates and helmets. Their vessels were decorated with flags and streamers, so that the whole made a grand and noble appearance such as was never seen before at sea."

Cook then sailed the *Resolution* back to New Zealand to try to find out what had happened to the *Adventure*. He heard that some of the crew had been killed and eaten by the Maoris, and Lieutenant Furneaux had then set sail for England via Cape Horn and the Atlantic. The *Adventure* thus completed the first circumnavigation of the world, traveling from west to east.

Cook, in the *Resolution*, followed the same course, and discovered the South Atlantic island of South Georgia on the way. He reached England once more in July 1775.

Last voyage

The success of Cook's second expedition brought him more honors and awards. He was elected a Fellow of the Royal Society for his services to science, presented to King George III, and promoted to the rank of captain.

Cook now hoped to settle down at home; but this was still not to be. By sailing right across the areas where it was supposed to be, Cook had proved that *Terra Australis* did not exist. But there was now talk of a new attempt to find a northwest passage. For two hundred years, explorers had been searching for a sea passage across the top of North America that would link the Atlantic

Cook was honored for his navigational work and was presented to King George III.

The headquarters of the Royal Society, situated at Crane Court, London, until 1782.

Ocean with the Pacific. They had all started by sailing from Europe, northwestward across the Atlantic, to the coast of Labrador. The new plan was to start from the opposite direction, sailing north across the Pacific. If there were such a passage, it might be easier to find that way.

There was keen commercial interest in such a search. Merchant ships sailing between Europe and the Far East had to navigate right across the Indian Ocean, around the Cape of Good Hope, and continue up the whole length of Africa. A route around the top of North America would save them both time and money.

Cook was now 47 years old, and tired after the years of travel and the responsibilities of command. He had also fallen seriously ill during the second expedition. Nevertheless, he volunteered to lead a new expedition to look for a northwest passage, and the Admiralty accepted his offer.

Back to Polynesia

In 1776, Captain Cook went to sea again. His own ship, the *Resolution*, was joined this time by the *Discovery*. Two other famous mariners sailed with him; William Bligh, who later faced mutiny as captain on HMS *Bounty*, and George Vancouver, who gave his name to the large island and city on Canada's Pacific coast.

The expedition went first to New Zealand – where Cook was pleased to note that seeds planted on earlier visits had grown into healthy crops – and then proceeded yet again to Tahiti for ship repairs and rest.

Sailing north from there, they crossed the equator and

discovered Christmas Island, which they sighted on Christmas Eve, 1777. Early in 1778, they arrived at an important group of islands. As Cook's log records, the natives welcomed them even more warmly than the Tahitians. "Canoes came off from the shore and brought with them roasting pigs and some very fine potatoes. Once again we found ourselves in the land of plenty."

From where they anchored, they could see smoking volcanoes in the distance. On going ashore, they were amazed at the images of the local war gods. Some were carved from tree trunks and were about twice the height of a man;

Hawaiian canoes drawn by a member of Cook's expedition.

others were made of feathers, teeth and pearls. All of them looked most fierce.

Cook had discovered the Hawaiian Islands, which he named the Sandwich Islands, after the Earl of Sandwich, First Lord of the Admiralty.

Land of totems, forest and snow

In March 1778, Cook and his crews reached the Pacific coast of North America (or New Albion as it was then known). He devoted several pages of his log to the local Indians. He described their style of headdress decorated with large feathers, and how they covered their bodies with oily red paint. "Their faces," he added, "are often stained a white color. This gives them a ghastly

Cook and his crews traded with the Indians they met in North America.

The Resolution *and* Discovery *were trapped in the ice of the Bering Sea.*

aspect." Their canoes also caught Cook's attention. One of them "was remarkable for a singular head, which had a bird's eye and bill, of enormous size, painted on it." Landing parties from the *Resolution* and the *Discovery* saw the same strange bird, together with many other images, on the Indians' tall totem poles. A brisk trade soon developed, with the Indians offering the furs of bears, wolves, foxes, deer, racoons and polecats, in exchange for knives, chisels, nails, buttons and small mirrors.

Cook followed and charted the coast north and west around Alaska, looking in vain for a break in the great line of pine forests and snow-capped mountains. His ships passed into the Bering Sea, named after the Danish explorer Vitus Bering, who fifty years before had first sailed into it. They pressed on, through the Bering Strait which separates Alaska from Asia, and this time crossed the Arctic Circle. They met fog, sleet and snowstorms, and were finally halted by a wall of ice, just as they had been in the Antarctic.

It was now the end of August 1778. Winter was approaching in those far northern climes, and the *Resolution* had sprung several leaks. Cook sought refuge in Unalaska, a Russian trading post on the chilly Aleutian Islands, and there he carried emergency repairs as best he could.

Death in Hawaii

Disappointed at not finding a northwest passage, Cook returned to the Hawaiian Islands. But thefts of the explorers' property by the islanders and some unpleasant quarrels ruined the visit.

Everyone was relieved when they set sail again. However, the *Resolution* was damaged in a storm, and both ships returned to Hawaii for more repairs. It proved to be a fateful move. While the *Discovery* was at anchor, the natives stole her cutter. On the morning of February 14, 1779, Cook angrily led an armed party ashore. There was a fight on the beach. Cook was surrounded by warriors, struck down and slaughtered.

A day or two later, fellow officers recovered his remains and gave him a burial at sea with full naval honors. The expedition then sailed back to the Bering Sea, in another attempt to find a northwest passage. They failed,

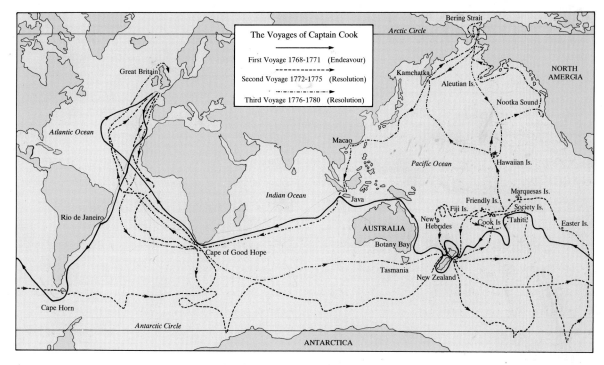

The Voyages of Captain Cook

First Voyage 1768-1771 (Endeavour)
Second Voyage 1772-1775 (Resolution)
Third Voyage 1776-1780 (Resolution)

Captain James Cook made three major voyages, which took him all over the globe. He came across many lands that were previously unknown to Europeans.

and finally reached England in October 1780, after four long years at sea.

The name of Captain James Cook is commemorated across the length and breadth of the vast Pacific – Cook Strait and Mount Cook, New Zealand; Cooktown and Cook's Passage, Australia; the Cook Islands, Polynesia; Cook Inlet, Alaska. Cook charted the greater part of the world's largest ocean, its far-flung coasts, and its thousands of islands and atolls. With his discoveries and surveys, the geography of the world was very nearly complete. Only Antarctica remained to be discovered.

Cook was not only a superb navigator and explorer. He was a stern but humane commander, and unlike many naval officers of his time, put the health and safety of his crews before his own. By doing so much to eradicate scurvy, he saved the lives of many of the men who sailed with him, and thousands more in years to come.

Important dates

1728   James Cook born in Marton-in-Cleveland, Yorkshire, England (October 27).

1746   Goes to sea as apprentice on a Whitby collier.

1755   Joins the Navy, as an able seaman.

1759   Is promoted to master on HMS *Pembroke* and plays an important part in the British capture of Quebec during the Seven Years War.

1768   Commissioned as a lieutenant and sails on the *Endeavour* on his first voyage of exploration to search for *Terra Australis*.

1769–70   Arrives at Tahiti in the Pacific, and makes astronomical observations. Charts all the New Zealand coastline, the east coast of Australia and the Great Barrier Reef. Is nearly shipwrecked.

1771   Departs on second voyage of exploration with the *Resolution* and *Adventure*. Second attempt to find *Terra Australis*, and also tests newly-invented chronometer as a navigational aid.

1771–74   Crosses the Antarctic Circle twice, and charts many Pacific islands, including Easter Island, and the Fiji and New Hebrides island groups.

1775   Returns home again and is promoted to rank of captain.

1776   Sails on third voyage of exploration with the *Resolution* and *Discovery* to search for a northwest passage.

1777–78   Discovers Christmas Island, the Hawaiian island group, charts the Pacific coast of North America from Oregon to Alaska, and crosses the Arctic Circle.

1779   Returns from the Arctic to Hawaii for repairs to ships. Is involved in dispute with natives, and killed (February 14).

1780   His expedition makes one more attempt to find a northwest passage before returning to England.

Books to read

Day, Grove D. *Captain Cook*. Honolulu, HI: Hogarth Press, 1977.

Harley, Ruth. *Captain James Cook, revised edition*. Mahwah, NJ: Troll Associates, 1979.

Hoobler, Dorothy and Thomas. *The Voyages of Captain Cook*. New York: Putnam Publishing Group, 1983.

Peach, L. Dugarde. *The Story of Captain Cook*. Bedford Hills, NY: Merry Thoughts.

Sylvester, David W. *Captain Cook and the Pacific*. White Plains, NY: Longman, 1971.

Glossary

Admiralty   The government department responsible for the British Royal Navy.

Antarctic Circle   An imaginary circle around the earth, parallel to the equator, at latitude 66° 32′ south.

Arctic Circle   An imaginary circle around the earth, parallel to the equator, at latitude 66° 32′ north.

Astronomers   Scientists who study stars and other heavenly bodies.

Atolls   Circular coral reefs, or strings of coral islands surrounding lagoons.

Botanists   Scientists who study plant life.

Charting   Mapping coastlines in detail for navigational purposes.

Chronometer   A timepiece designed to be accurate in all conditions of temperature and movement, used especially at sea.

Circumnavigation   Traveling completely around the world.

Commission   A document giving a specific rank to an officer in the armed forces.

Cutter   A ship's boat, powered by oars or sails, for carrying light cargo or passengers.

Eclipse   Total or partial obscuring of one heavenly body by another.

Equator   An imaginary line around the earth, halfway between the North and South Poles.

Hemisphere   Half of the earth; divided into the Northern and Southern Hemisphere.

Log   A daily record of a ship's progress, kept by the captain.

Navigation   The process of planning a route and directing a ship.

Objective   An aim or purpose.

Outrigger canoes   Canoes with floats attached, to give them better stability.

Scurvy   A serious disease caused by lack of vitamin C. Many sailors used to suffer from scurvy because of the shortage of fresh fruit and vegetables in a normal ship's diet.

Strait   A narrow body of water linking two larger ones.

Transit   The route of a star or planet, as seen from the earth.

Zoologists   Scientists who study animal life.

Index